D1607267

ON A MISSION

FBI Agent

ON A MISSION

Bomb Squad Technician

Border Security

Dogs on Patrol

FBI Agent

Fighter Pilot

Firefighter

Paramedic

Search and Rescue Team

Secret Service Agent

Special Forces

SWAT Team

Undercover Police Officer

ON A MISSION

FBI Agent

By Tim Newcomb

Mason Crest
450 Parkway Drive, Suite D
Broomall, PA 19008
www.masoncrest.com

Printed and bound in the United States of America.

Series ISBN: 978-1-4222-3391-7
Hardback ISBN: 978-1-4222-3394-8
EBook ISBN: 978-1-4222-8503-9

First printing
1 3 5 7 9 8 6 4 2

Produced by Shoreline Publishing Group LLC
Santa Barbara, California
Editorial Director: James Buckley Jr.
Designer: Bill Madrid
Production: Sandy Gordon
www.shorelinepublishing.com
Cover Photo: Larry Kim

Library of Congress Cataloging-in-Publication Data

Newcomb, Tim, 1978-
        FBI agent / by Tim Newcomb.
                pages cm. -- (On a mission!)
        Includes index.
            ISBN 978-1-4222-3394-8 (hardback : alk. paper) -- ISBN 978-1-4222-3391-7 (series : alk. paper)
-- ISBN 978-1-4222-8503-9 (ebook) 1. United States. Federal Bureau of Investigation--Juvenile literature.
2. Criminal investigation--United States--Juvenile literature. 3. Law enforcement--United States--Juvenile
literature. I. Title.
 HV8144.F43N47 2016
 363.25023'73--dc23
                                            2015004841

Contents

Key Icons to Look For

Words to Understand: These words with their easy-to-understand definitions will increase the reader's understanding of the text, while building vocabulary skills.

Sidebars: This boxed material within the main text allows readers to build knowledge, gain insights, explore possibilities, and broaden their perspectives by weaving together additional information to provide realistic and holistic perspectives.

Research Projects: Readers are pointed toward areas of further inquiry connected to each chapter. Suggestions are provided for projects that encourage deeper research and analysis.

Text-Dependent Questions: These questions send the reader back to the text for more careful attention to the evidence presented here.

Series Glossary of Key Terms: This back-of-the-book glossary contains terminology used throughout this series. Words found here increase the reader's ability to read and comprehend higher-level books and articles in this field.

Emergency!

A discovery by some curious boys in the woods led the FBI to one of the most notorious bank robbers of all-time.

On a clear, spring day, a group of boys playing in the woods in Pennsylvania dug up a long, plastic pipe. It wasn't the buried treasure that boys often dream of finding, but it turned out to be one that delighted the Federal Bureau of Investigation—the FBI.

Friday evening was usually a time of the week that bank workers looked forward to. It was the end of the week, the end of work. The weekend was often just moments away from starting. For more than 30 years, however, Friday evenings in East Coast states—from Virginia into New England—provided a little extra scare for bank workers.

Friday evening was when Friday Night Freddy struck to rob banks. He did it quickly—and he was armed.

The FBI was on the case because bank robbery is a **federal** crime, which is one of the things that the FBI is responsible for investigating. FBI personnel had searched and searched for Friday Night Freddy, even pinpointing the way he robbed the banks, the same way every time. They weren't having any luck, though. Friday Night Freddy was getting away with his crime over and over.

Words to Understand

federal related to the government of the United States, as opposed to the government of an individual state or city

ninja a type of ancient Japanese warrior, skilled at fighting, but also at gymnastic, martial-arts moves

spree a series of events done rapidly in a short period of time

7

Every holdup was the same. He would charge into a bank, usually just minutes before they were closing on Friday evenings. That was the time when the bank had the most cash on hand, and when workers were busy with trying to close up shop and plan their weekends. When he came in, he certainly didn't come unannounced.

He wore giant clothes, big and baggy. That made it hard to tell exactly how tall or heavy he was. He also wore a Halloween mask on every job. He didn't always wear the same mask, but almost every one was scary. His favorite, though, was one that looked like movie bad guy Freddy Krueger; that mask and his choice of "work day" gave him his nickname.

Friday Night Freddy would make his way into the bank, waving a gun around, demanding all the workers lie on the floor. Nobody was likely to argue with a man in a scary mask and holding a gun. Twice, he shot people during robbery attempts, once by accident and once when someone was not following his orders. (Both people recovered.)

Then, when everyone was down, Friday Night Freddy would perform a little **ninja**-style robbery. He would get low and then jump—almost like a ninja—over the counters to where the employees worked. Using heavy-duty bags that could carry plenty of weight without ripping, he'd fill the bags with as much cash as he could find. He knew where to look, too, finding even the spots that most bank robbers don't know about.

Friday Night Freddy moved fast, not wasting any time. When he was ready to leave, he did so just as quickly, sprinting back out of the bank in a hurry. The entire robbery usually took less than two minutes.

However, what made this bank robber different from all the others was the way he got away. Most bank robbers work with someone else. Usually they have a partner either inside the bank to keep an eye on people and watch for police, or

Friday Night Freddy wore a mask like this one, modeled after a famous horror-movie villain.

outside waiting in a car ready to screech away. Friday Night Freddy had neither.

The bank robber worked alone. He didn't use a car to get away. He ran.

Not limiting his crime **spree** to just one state or city, Friday Night Freddy pinpointed the location of the bank he was going to rob to only those near forests. Without a car to flee in and only his feet to carry him, Freddy always ran into the woods, seemingly to vanish. In reality, Friday Night Freddy was stashing his cash—and anything else that could trace him to the robbery—in a place in

Police looked for evidence after each robbery, but Freddy left behind few clues to his identity.

the woods that he already had scouted out, such as the one the teenagers stumbled upon. Then he would hop on a dirt bike that would take him miles away from the evidence. He would come back several days later to pick up the loot.

Robbing banks only in the late fall, winter, and early spring meant that it started getting dark early in the evening. So when the Friday-night bank robber ran, he had the extra cover of darkness to keep him hidden.

Friday Night Freddy robbed in New England and Virginia, but Pennsylvania was where he hit the most. Over 30 years, he robbed nearly 50 banks, taking with him close to $2 million. All in cash. All in bags. All into the woods never to be seen again. Still, the FBI was on the case…and the FBI never gives up.

Later, in the final chapter "Mission Accomplished," find out how the FBI finally tracked down this elusive robber. First, learn more about the hard-working members of the FBI.

FBI Special Agents are trained for investigation or law enforcement, and are ready to deal with any threat.

Chapter 1

Mission Prep

While different people who have jobs in many law-enforcement departments are called agents, people who work for the FBI are called Special Agents.

There is no such thing as a typical day for an FBI Special Agent. One day a Special Agent could be **testifying** in a federal court, and the next out gathering evidence on a bank robbery. FBI agents do everything from researching crime, working with other agencies on finding the information to make an arrest, or even working on their own in an office. However, the quiet work of finding information is put aside when it's time to get into action to take part in a raid, go into the field to track a suspect, or even take down one of the famous "Most Wanted."

The FBI is responsible for enforcing federal laws. With more than 300 different areas that the FBI keeps in line, an FBI Special Agent can

Words to Understand

corruption the illegal acts by people in elected or appointed public offices

counterintelligence the process of seeking information about other nations' possible acts against your own nation

surveillance the act of watching another person or a place, usually from a hidden location

testifying speaking under oath during a court trial

work in a wide variety of fields, everything from computer crimes to financial crime and from bank robbery to finding criminals on the run. Most of the crimes that the FBI handles are those that cross state lines. This helps to avoid confusion between neighboring states. When a crime goes national, the FBI is set up to handle the job.

Five Areas of Expertise

To get started, the FBI requires that each new special agent qualify for work under one of its key areas of responsibility. Those include accounting, computer science and information technology, language, and law. Each one of these programs includes "critical skills" needed to excel as an FBI Special Agent. That means that anyone looking to work for the FBI already has to have some background in one of those areas. Applicants must have completed a four-year degree from a college or university and held an office job for at least three years. For example, you don't move into the FBI after working in a restaurant or selling auto supplies. Aiming for the FBI means having expertise and experience suited to the work of the agency.

The FBI focuses its special agents on five career paths: intelligence (looking for information about crime and criminals); counterintelligence (preventing someone from attacking the United States or getting information from the U.S. intelligence community); counterterrorism (working against terrorists trying to harm the United States); criminal work (such as bank robberies or kidnappings); or cybercrime (crimes done using computers). Based on a special agent's abilities and education, along with his or her ability to master certain subjects, the FBI puts agents in the positions that will best help the agency and the country.

Agents in intelligence find useful and timely information that can help protect the nation from threats. In **counterintelligence**, the FBI works to keep foreign attacks from hurting the United States or its government agencies. Sometimes that means stopping spies trying to steal secret information. Secrets could be almost anything—a military plan that could harm a U.S. warship or a new technology that could be used to harm Americans. The counterintelligence program is involved in figuring it all out. Sometimes the FBI partners with the Central Intelligence Agency (CIA), which works outside the United States, so they can work together to create the best counterintelligence and keep out the threats.

The counterterrorism division looks to disrupt and dismantle any terrorist groups working within the United States. Much of this work is done in secret so the enemies do not find out about the investigation until it is too late. Agents in this area often have to work undercover and are experts in foreign languages and cultures.

The criminal investigative division takes a different path. It looks into financial crime, violent crime, public **corruption**, civil-rights violations, drug-related crimes, and more. Finally, the cyber division focuses on crimes that occur with computers, looking to stop criminals hoping to hurt people or steal money.

A Nation of Agents

The FBI has "field offices" within the United States and in many foreign countries. Each helps out in one of the agency's five key areas. With 56 field offices and headquarters in Washington, D.C., there's always a place for a new Special Agent.

The FBI was founded in 1908, when the U.S. government decided it needed help investigating crime. Under President Theodore Roosevelt, a group of agents was chosen to work in the

FBI Headquarters in Washington, D.C., is home to the FBI Director and hundreds of Special Agents and staff.

An Agent in Action

FBI Special Agent Henry Holden tells the story of one senior agent who was following a suspect about to leave the country. This agent was watching the suspect in an airport. The suspect was buying different plane tickets to confuse trackers. The agent followed him to a gate and let other agents know via radio which plane the suspect got on, allowing the agents to be ready when the plane landed. While being followed, the suspect started looking at the agent more and more. That could have led to a dangerous scene. In order to keep everyone safe and make the suspect feel comfortable enough to get on the plane, the agent pretended to be waiting for a friend who had just gotten off a plane. He started talking to this perfect stranger. It worked, and this surveillance allowed the FBI to arrest the suspect when he landed at his destination.

Department of Justice. In 1910, that group officially became the Bureau of Investigation. Since 1935, it has been called the FBI. Today, the FBI is one of the largest law-enforcement agencies in the world, with more than 12,000 Special Agents, along with thousands more people working to provide the agents with support and information. The FBI also has offices around the world to coordinate with similar law-enforcement agencies.

All of these people are working toward the same mission: protecting the United States and its citizens. One of the most common ways to do this is by interviewing people and getting them to tell agents information. Another key part of the job is undercover **surveillance**.

In order to find new information, agents watch other people. They do it undercover, though, meaning they can't be seen. This type of work requires technology to help the agents see and hear when they aren't right next to the person, but it also requires patience. Agents need to be willing to spend many hours gathering information, but they must also be able to spring into action quickly if they need to arrest a criminal or stop a crime.

Text-Dependent Questions

1. Name three of the five areas that the FBI investigates.
2. What are the two ways FBI agents use most to gather information?
3. What is the difference between intelligence and counterintelligence?

Research Project

Find an area within the FBI that interests you and research more about that particular job.

Chapter 2

This is a training exercise that teaches Special Agents how to work together to capture a barricaded suspect.

Training Mind and Body

Every FBI Special Agent knows all about Quantico, Virginia, the home of the FBI Academy. The career of every FBI Special Agent starts with 21 weeks of intensive training at this facility. Students live on campus and spend time in the classroom studying a wide variety of subjects. They also leave the classroom for physical training that covers self-defense, combat skills, and the use of firearms.

Getting through the academy, located near a U.S. Marine base about an hour south of Washington, D.C., isn't easy—but having the job of an FBI Special Agent was not designed to be easy. Trainees must pass multiple tests, both in the classroom and in physical fitness. The training must reflect the unpredictability of an FBI Special Agent's role. Agents

Words to Understand

ethics the ideas and rules that lead a person to make the right choices

mentor to guide and lead a person who is new to a particular job or career

search warrant an official document that law enforcement personnel must get from a judge before they can conduct a search might study **ethics** in the morning and then get down on the ground and learn how to properly shoot a pistol in the afternoon.

Learning to Make Good Choices

Training the mind in the classroom and the body with physical exercise aren't always separate. That is where "situational training" comes in. In this special kind of "classroom," the new special agents are placed in a spot where they have to make quick decisions. These decisions are similar to the ones they would face in the real world. For example, on a shooting range, a fake criminal might pop up out of nowhere. The agent-in-training needs to make a quick decision on how to handle the situation to protect the most people. Practicing at a training center gives the agents a lot of different chances to make the right decision. Training also helps agents learn from their mistakes. FBI Special Agents spend many weeks in situational training. They learn from mistakes and figure out the best approach.

Senior Special Agent Terry Royster works for the FBI's New Agent & Analysts Training Unit. She says that recruits in the program—about 50 at a time—will spend more time working on their mind than their body. However, they still do both.

Special Agents learn the safe way to make an arrest, as shown in this training photo.

Nonverbal Signals

Unfortunately, people lie all the time, especially to FBI Special Agents. One way to tell if someone is speaking the truth or telling a lie is to see what they are saying with their body. These are called nonverbal signals. Agents must learn to read clues from the people they are talking to in order to discover if they are telling the truth. For example, right-handed people will often look to the left when they are thinking of a truthful answer and look toward the right when they are making something up. FBI agents look for these small clues. There are plenty of other clues as well, such as someone wanting to turn away from the agent, getting nervous or not keeping eye contact with the agent. All these nonverbal signals can help an FBI Special Agent figure out the truth.

"We are more of a thinking agency," she says. "Part of it is learning how to be an agent."

Agents need to know how to do everything from interviewing or interrogating a suspect to learning all the laws they have to follow during an investigation. They are taught about rules and regulations, but they are also taught how to do the job.

It Starts in Class

Not every training situation requires student agents to decide if they should shoot a gun. As part of investigations, FBI Special Agents have plenty of rules they need to follow. That is why the classroom work is so important. Some of that classroom work spills over into the physical work. For example, if Special Agents need to conduct a search of a suspect's house, they must follow the rules to get a **search warrant**. Once they have that warrant, though, they will have to go to the suspect's house and actually search it. Nobody enjoys having his house searched. Because it is the job of an FBI Special Agent to find out if a suspect is breaking the law, the agents must be ready for anything when they get to a house.

The training helps the agents do that, all with specialized situations. Agent Royster says the new agents do a lot of role playing. They start with small tasks and work up to complicated ones. She says that knowing the classroom part of the information is one thing, but going out into the real world and trying it is completely different.

Graduation from the FBI Academy doesn't mean agents stop learning. After graduation, the agents' first assignment generally places them in a field office for about three years. During that time, they are paired with a veteran special agent whose goal is to **mentor** them and help them apply the lessons learned at the FBI Academy. Once the initial three years are up, the agents might move to a larger field office or to a different part of the agency. The more experiences Special Agents can receive early in their career, the more they will learn what areas may fit them best.

Firearm Safety and More

While training, agents spend a lot of time working with firearms. Two days a week for four hours each, student agents practice to become safe and smart with guns of different types. Agents start out learning safety techniques, and build up to become skilled at shooting everything from pistols to rifles to shotguns.

Combat courses teach the agents when to shoot and when to use other self-defense tools, placing them in all types of situations. The on-site training includes sessions in which fake people pop up, some with a gun and some without. The agent trainees have to figure out the right way to react—to shoot or not to shoot. By starting small and working into more complicated scenarios, the agents learn to use their mind quickly and let their body follow. The training is designed so agents don't have to think about what to do; they react automatically, which saves time and lives. Often knowing when to shoot is more important than actually pulling the trigger.

All FBI Special Agents have to be experts at marksmanship. They practice on the range and also have to learn to use different weapons.

Once agents master the basics, training gets more complicated. Instructors send the agents on fake cases outside the training academy, using actors in the real world. Agents have to know how to write up an investigation plan, research the case, and follow through on their assignment. With role players acting along, the agents have to knock on doors and make quick decisions, putting to use information about interviewing techniques and what the law says about each situation.

While working as an FBI Special Agent, agents continue to learn and earn specialized skills. The FBI covers so many areas of investigation that it needs people to understand everything from taking apart bombs to the dangers of chemicals and the secrets of forgery.

Some agents take advanced driving courses. This teaches them how to handle a car, truck, or motorcycle during a chase, or to evade a pursuing vehicle.

Other agents begin, or expand on, language courses. With the international work against terrorism, being able to communicate with experts around the world is more crucial than ever. Agents can learn more about cyber crimes involving computers, combining their law-enforcement expertise with "white-hat" hacking skills.

All through their time as agents, FBI agents can take classes and attend seminars that teach all sorts of special techniques and new laws. The learning that started at the FBI Academy never ends, even for the most seasoned of agents.

Text-Dependent Questions

1. What are some things agents learn at the FBI Academy?
2. What can agents learn once they've graduated from the academy?
3. Give an example of classroom training combined with physical training.

Research Project

Investigate the FBI Academy and find something students learn there that isn't included in this book.

At the FBI lab, a tiny drop of blood such as this can be the key that unlocks the answer to a mystery.

Chapter 3

Tools and Technology

FBI Special Agents rely on their mental and physical training, and on the support of agents working around them, but that teamwork can only take them so far. Agents need tools and technology to put their plans into action or to gather the information they need to make arrests. The FBI is a world leader in the use of technology to fight and prevent crime, using science to do everything from defusing bombs to tracking DNA to identifying suspects from fingerprints. Here's a look at some of the tech used by the FBI today.

A Bomb Library?

Not every office building contains a bomb library. The FBI has one, though—the Terrorist Explosive Device Analytical Center (TEDAC). Located at the FBI laboratory in Virginia, the site of the FBI

Words to Understand

biometrics the science of using information unique to each person to identify an individual

cryptography another word for writing in code

forensic having to do with crime-scene evidence

racketeering a type of crime in which criminals work together to create networks with illegal goals

Academy, TEDAC is a bomb library that helps the FBI and other agencies fight terrorism.

Whether bombs come from the battlefields of Afghanistan or from the streets of a U.S. city, the pieces of the bomb are sent to TEDAC for FBI agents to analyze and record. Agents have examined more than 100,000 bombs since TEDAC was created in 2003. They use **forensic** evidence—DNA, fingerprints, and **biometrics** (a way of measuring any biological data found on the bomb)—to identify the bomb maker and see if the bomb is similar to others already found. Using what the agents find out, they can create detailed intelligence reports that may help predict future bomb attacks and save lives.

The FBI Lab

The FBI crime laboratory started as the Technical Crime Lab in 1932, and has now grown to house 500 scientific experts and Special Agents working on a variety of research, not all related to bombs. The FBI lab works on code breaking, firearms identification, and DNA analysis, among other areas.

One of the easiest ways to conceal information is to write in code. Criminals share information they don't want anyone else to know. Entire governments use codes to hide their communication. The FBI has a plan for all that. The **Racketeering** Records Analysis Unit works out of the FBI laboratory to crack all different kinds of **cryptography** (secret writing). Whether cipher systems (letters or numbers arranged differently) or codes (any symbols used to replace words), the team uses computers, math, and experience to crack codes.

If every gun tells a story, the FBI's firearms collection could fill a large book. With more than 7,000 different firearms collected since 1932, the FBI lab has just about every make and model of gun ever made. Firearm experts can use the collection as a hands-on reference catalog. When analysts need to study, take apart, reassemble, or test fire a gun as part of an investigation, they have what they need already in the lab. Every gun has a unique way of shooting a bullet, so using technology to test fire the guns produces plenty of information.

"Often, this collection is used in active cases in comparing known samples from our collection with question samples from the field," says John Webb, a firearms examiner in the lab's Firearms/Toolmarks Unit. "Often, an investigator will receive a part of a firearm or a firearm that isn't functional. We can take that and compare it with our reference collection, determine what isn't functioning, and repair it so we can obtain the test fire we need to conduct examinations with bullets."

By comparing bullets used in a crime with a gun found on a suspect, the FBI can connect criminals with their crimes, using science and its own collective expertise.

Tracking People

Science has provided law enforcement with a very valuable tool. You may know from crime TV shows that everyone's DNA is unique, but that's not all.

WELCOME
TO
HOGAN'S ALLEY
CITY   LIMITS

CAUTION: LAW ENFORCEMENT TRAINING EXERCISES IN PROGRESS. DISPLAY OF WEAPONS FIRING OF BLANK AMMUNITION AND ARRESTS MAY OCCUR. IF CHALLENGED PLEASE FOLLOW INSTRUCTIONS.

HAVE A NICE DAY

The science of biometrics has expanded beyond DNA to help identify suspects. The FBI uses the Combined DNA Index System (CODIS). It compares DNA profiles to help solve crimes. How does this happen? A forensic laboratory receives evidence that may have DNA on it. The lab enters the DNA profile into CODIS to compare it to profiles from around the country. Often a previously unknown DNA profile will connect to a known criminal.

Using DNA and CODIS, FBI scientists even use microscopic hair analysis. Cases with hair evidence recovered from a crime scene are compared with other known hair samples. Miniscule pieces of hair fall from us all the time. Being able to properly identify that hair can help in solving crimes.

All this information continues to give the FBI new tools to fight crime. In 2014, the FBI opened a new center that combines all this science in one system. It's a biometrics data center called the Next Generation Identification System. Agencies

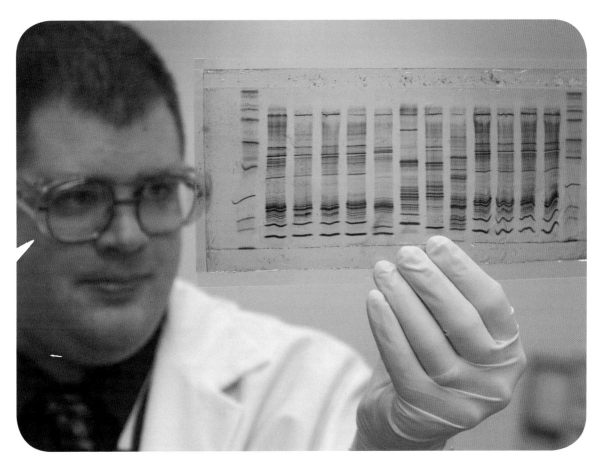

searching the FBI's criminal history record database for matches to various subjects now get a
faster and more accurate response.

Another part of the lab handles everything
from the science of chemical or nuclear weapons to crime scene documentation. The experts
that gather the evidence used in these areas are

**Scientific
investigation, such as
using DNA to identify
suspects, is more
important than ever
to FBI agents.**

FBI agents are not afraid to get their hands dirty, digging out evidence wherever they find it.

called Evidence Response Team Units. Such units include mechanical engineers, forensic specialists, and analysts, and they focus on finding as much crime-scene evidence as possible. Special teams are even called in for such things as underwater evidence response. There, diving teams use sophisticated equipment to locate and recover evidence. Just because you work in a lab for the FBI doesn't mean you won't be out in the field, doing the dirty work.

Text-Dependent Questions

1. In what year did the FBI lab open?
2. What sort of evidence is examined at TEDAC?
3. What do FBI students learn when working in Hogan's Alley?

Research Project

Find a famous criminal case solved by the FBI and explain what parts of the FBI lab could have been used to help solve the crime.

POLICE LINE DO NOT CROSS

Chapter 4

The Pennsylvania woods became a crime scene when FBI Special Agents discovered evidence that led to a bank robber.

Mission Accomplished!

The buried treasure a pair of boys found in the woods outside of Philadelphia on April Fools' Day was no joke. The boys discovered a three-foot-long piece of PVC pipe tucked inside a ditch. The pipe was covered on both ends, making it a mystery.

After clearing away one cap, the boys didn't find any sort of treasure they were looking for, but it proved a treasure the FBI so dearly wanted. Inside were five guns, five hundred bullets, notes on which banks along the East Coast were easy targets to rob, eight Halloween masks, and hand-drawn maps.

These weren't just regular maps. They included odd sayings, such as "Carbon W" and "Ca$he," with all sorts of lines for small roads, large boulders, strange trees, and distances between these landmarks.

The boys did the right thing and handed the pipe over to the police. The FBI had it by the next day. Right away, the FBI knew it had a good lead on Friday Night Freddy.

Words to Understand

theorized created a possible scenario or answer based on the available evidence

The FBI agents started with the maps, which marked key locations of hidden items. Agents tracked the locations and found small, hand-dug bunkers scattered throughout the mountains near Pennsylvania. During the search, agents found 30 guns, thousands of bullets, Halloween masks, makeup, climbing gear, financial records, and even $47,000 in cash.

Also included in the "buried treasure" were Ninja training books from the 1980s, including *The Mystic Art of the Ninja, Ninjutsu*: *The Art of the Invisible Warrior*, and *Night Fighter's Handbook*. With this information on hand, the FBI knew they were on the trail of the Friday-night bank robber. The most important clue was a simple advertisement. A lone piece of paper from a karate studio in Drexel Hill, Pa., proved to be the key in helping the FBI chase down Friday Night Freddy.

At the karate-training studio, FBI agents asked the owner about any middle-aged students in incredible shape. The owner had an answer right away: Carl Gugasian.

With a name, it was only a matter of time before the FBI was able to move closer, step by step. Using database records, the FBI located Gugasian's apartment, which was near the buried

Friday Night Freddy obviously had some martial arts training . . . and the FBI used that clue to track him down.

Changing Focus

Ever since the terrorist attacks on September 11, 2001, the FBI has put a renewed focus on terrorism—finding and stopping the people seeking to harm the United States. FBI Special Agents are actively investigating terrorists in the United States and internationally, using the information they gather to stop attacks and terrorist plans. Doing this means a group of agents must be able to use new technology and work with new groups. Changing the focus of the terrorism group within the FBI required the ability to train and learn on the job. Being able to grow and improve at any point is the most important aspect of training.

pipe containing the initial clues. The FBI soon learned that Gugasian was a third-degree karate black belt and an Army veteran with plenty of training in engineering, and that locals commonly saw him jogging with a weighted backpack. The agents **theorized** that the robber was training to carry heavy amounts of money during his escapes.

Research into the suspect showed that the car he drove wasn't very nice, but that he did have $500,000 in the bank. He claimed to work as a gambler and business consultant. Gugasian also spent plenty of time at the Philadelphia Free Library, a perfect place to look at maps and to help plan his next bank robbery.

Nearly a year after the discovery of the pipe, FBI Special Agents arrested Gugasian near the library. Gugasian quickly confessed to the entire string of crimes. He even led officers to other places where he stashed items from the robberies. He told officials that he started robbing banks as a teenager and couldn't get himself out of it. He was sentenced to 17 years in prison, but his good behavior ever since his arrest and in prison—he even agreed to make a bank robbery training video for the FBI—may get him out of prison early.

This older photo shows Gugasian before he began his crime spree.

If he does get out early, though, the FBI won't have to worry. Gugasian won't have any of his old habits to fall back on. All his buried treasure has been dug up. He certainly won't have any more scary Friday Night Freddy masks to wear, either. The FBI took care of that.

Find Out More

Books

Bhattacharjee, Yudhijit. "How the FBI Cracked a Chinese Spy Ring." *The New Yorker Magazine*, May 12, 2014.

Fish, Jacqueline and the FBI. *FBI Handbook of Crime Scene Forensics.* New York: Skyhorse Publishing, 2015.

Streissguth, Tom. *The Security Agencies of the United States*. New York: Enslow Publishers, 2012.

Wong, Adam. *Careers in the FBI.* London: Cavendish Square Publishing, 2014.

Web Sites

www.fbi.gov   The official site of the FBI includes information on its agents, its role in law enforcement, and its history. Search the site for its Teen Academy program.

Series Glossary of Key Terms

apprehending capturing and arresting someone who has committed a crime

assassinate kill somebody, especially a political figure

assessment the act of gathering information and making a decision about a particular topic

contraband material that is illegal to possess

cryptography another word for writing in code

deployed put to use, usually in a military or law-enforcement operation

dispatcher a person who announces emergencies over police radio and helps organize the efforts of first responders

elite among the very best; part of a select group of successful experts

evacuated moved to a safe location, away from danger

federal related to the government of the United States, as opposed to the government of an individual state or city

forensic having to do with crime scene evidence

instinctive based on natural impulse and done without instruction

interrogate to question a person as part of an official investigation

Kevlar an extra-tough fabric used in bulletproof vests

search-and-rescue the work of finding survivors after a disaster occurs, or the team that does this work

stabilize make steady or secure; also, in medicine, make a person safe to transport

surveillance the act of watching another person or a place, usually from a hidden location

trauma any physical injury to the body, usually involving bleeding

visa travel permit issued by a government to a citizen for a specific trip

warrant official document that allows the police to do something, such as arrest a person

Index

Photo Credits

Dreamstime.com: Uptail 6; Showface 30; Saniphoto 40; Arne9001 43.

Disguisetoi.fr: 9; Newscom/South Florida Sun-Sentinel/KRT/Judy Sloan Reich: 10.

Courtesy FBI: 12, 17, 20 (John B. Snyder), 23 (Chuck Kennedy), 27, 38; Sanders: 35; U.S. Customs and Border Protection: 37.

About the Author

Tim Newcomb is a freelance journalist based in the Pacific Northwest. He writes for *Sports Illustrated* and *Popular Mechanics* about sports design and engineering. His work has also appeared in *Time, Wired, Fast Company, Dwell, Stadia*, and a variety of publications around the world.

Dedicated to my daughters, Adia, Kalanie, and Rilanna, and the pursuit of their own missions!—T.N.